LOVE UNDEFINED

Poems

Jonathan Katz

C&R Press
Conscious & Responsible

Summer Tide Pool Chapbook
2016 Second Collection Selection 3 of 3 CB5

Printed in the United States of America

First Edition
1 2 3 4 5 6 7 8 9

Cover Design by Sally Underwood
Interior Design by Ali Chica

Library of Congress Cataloging-in-Publication Data

ISBN: 978-1-936196-56-2

C&R Press
Conscious & Responsible
www.crpress.org

For special discounted bulk purchases please contact:
C&R Press sales@crpress.org

Thank you to our generous Patreon patrons.

Golden speech should flower
From the soul so cherished,
And the mouth your kisses
Filled with fire.

-Sappho, Lyric LXXX
from Sappho; One Hundred Lyrics
by Bliss Carman

LOVE UNDEFINED

CONTENTS

To a Coy Friend on a Clear Night

Think how the moon and its chandelier of fragile constellations
descends into the wells of your eyes, shimmering in the deep mirrors,
a radiant pistil and innumerable glittering stamens.
Think also of the moon as a shiny, round tongue
lolling out of the night's throat
and of the brilliance of all the sharp, little teeth thus exposed.
This mouth is opening very slowly and among some billion tongues
amid a galaxy of teeth there will be a sudden great salivation
and a swallowing and a clamping closed again.
Kings and capitalists, colonels and dentists,
popes and churls and little girls
and all the bolus of this world will sink into eternity.
A yellow rose, the stars, this garden just behind us
and the sea itself are all seducers; all are brief.
Snakes are pastoral as flowers are
and peristalsis craws within as we through life,
but trees no less than sphincters give us metaphors
and I give these to you: how all our whispered words
are like an orchard hung with fruit;
how like a flaming apple is the sun;
how in the alchemist's fire the molten gold
runs like a universe aflow with pleasure;
how much like Paradise it is
to taste upon your lips the residue of kisses.

Bluets

As individual flowers the bluets are so inconspicuous
that few people notice them. But they colonize,
and vast patches of their white or pale lilac blossoms
are like frost on the grass in upland meadows.
They please the countryman, who may call them
quaker ladies innocence, though the individual
flower is only half an inch across its four small petals,
at the center of which is a golden eye.

This he reads in the spring in the New York Times
and wherever he goes thereafter he feels for
the golden eye watching him and
he is uneasily warm even in the gray rain,
even in the cloudy dusk, because he is afraid
of opening too soon or not at all
and everything perennial he knows depends on patience.

When they do meet, the tuber in his chest
knocks and thrashes about like a wild thing
in its hunger and she seems so unaware
and ordinary that a thousand flame-white doves
fly from his fingertips to their home
in the sun that beats down on them and she hardly
seems to notice, has merely smiled at him.

Later, picking any day like a petal,
thinking how to measure things that pass
and of their power, he wonders to himself
about her darkness and what,
etiolated and throbbing as it must have been,
drew her, like a stream from a high mountain place,
down to him.

High Noon Long Island

all the empty shells hold seas that whisper
if you can best leave the ones you want too much
your voice whispers in return becomes that stream
we followed over rocks through ferns and fallen
earthy cottonwood leaves toads silty pools turtles
to the shady bank where you told me
the other one you love is still a scarlet secret
you believe your father does not know
you'd packed an hourglass timed us
in innumerable grains made me so curious
but I have moved from where our Kansas was
have started over lying on the beach
this Long Island sun being nothing
like we knew so easy close my eyes and
I am lost in kissing someone I have found
the salty water in our mouths our ears
and on our tongues our glistening skin
nearby a stream cuts to the ocean
across the strand I hear the breeze
whisper through the sea-grape vines and cattails
your sand your sand is everywhere

Manhattan Project

There is no air moving.
You are looking at the deep, red carpeting.
The red alarm clock, the red chair,
the red bedspread, each red strand of red wire
in the red window-screen is tense at its edges.
I bomb your bourbon with a maraschino,
letting go its carmine stem.
You are thinking about ice cubes.
Outside, trees are clutching leaves and waiting.
Around our crystal tumblers' rims
a rosy red vermouth bouquet is rising.
I say your name.
Crows are calling.
My finger moves along your cherry lips.
Your breath is on my hands.
You look up.
A crow is flung away from its branch.
The branch is bleeding.
The sky is dark lime gelatin shimmering.
All the world is about to spin.

Miami

In the meat of the stone crab's cracked claw is a message.
Listen to it in the slow Morse code of the waves on the sand.
The optic nerve is a subtle fiber to the deep, clear waters of memory.
Fish the color of rainbows swim there,
the noon sun lambent on their glistening skin.
On the shore's damp skirt, sandpipers print their trident ideograms.

The evening's tide of revelers roiling along
the soft black asphalt of Calle Ocho
mimics migrations, past and future,
and a tongue of warm, wet air licks the lids of your eyes
with the promise of treasure, adventure, wild weather.

Put the fingers of your right hand on the left side of your neck.
Feel the pulse of your beating heart:
I will always be here for you
I will always be here for you
Miami flows within this blood
though sea floor crack and ocean flood
I will always be here for you
though sun turn silken cheek to clay
though all your roofs are blown away
I will always be here for you
For you I always will be here

The Orchid

lives on air,
by the most judgmental species
thought beautiful beyond compare;

and yet, so desperate for love,
she couples with a bee;
forgives the ardent bumbling of

the insect; sufficient to know him
a dazed fool, adoringly pitiful, and lucky
to have her in his poem.

Louche

Born literally Latin *luscus*,
she was blind in one eye.
Then she moves to France, changes her name
and her eyes cross.
It wasn't a pretty picture.
And yet,
she became so disreputable
no one even remembers her eyes.
Fishy, they say, if they know the ocean;
seedy, if they know the farm.
Some call that progress.
Others thought less of her.
How she survived
and was able to arouse desire,
one can only surmise.
Nevertheless, she leans against that street lamp,
ageless and *clichée*,
magnetic as judgment or blame,
and occupies a corner of your mind
that is not brightly lit.
You want to slap her
for her obvious disgrace, but
that expected cigarette between her lips
is offered for a flame.
You do provide it.
In exchange, she lets you see her face
and realize that what repulses you
was never in her eyes
but in the earnest question that she asks
of where her beauty lies.

Conundrum

Inconstant heart, conundrum, since I
cannot see within, my conscript spies
to know you are my hands and feet,
my scouting eyes report to them and fleet
as fingers tapping to a racing pulse are they,
defying my intended care and trust, betray
they must; though narrow quarters in the winding world
is sad, I'll see the traitor trapped within me, caged and curled.

Courage

There was that incident of the agency director
caught with the secretary *in flagrante delicto*
right there on the desk, papers and pens on the floor,
a position so shocking it could only be expressed
in florid Latin. Tawdry, my friends said, sleazy
and out of control, and I thought What energy,
What attraction, We're always talking about
how we want risk-takers; Well, that is what risk-taking
looks like, right? Sometimes you get caught with
your pants down taking risks, here's one:
Oh, I'm sure, Senator, my cousin is available for dinner,
or, Actually, Honey, I liked your hair better before.
Let's tell the foundation staff their idea is crappy,
low I.Q., our idea leverages more measureable
benefits, The rug label said "stain resistant" in Mandarin,
so, yeah, cabernet for about thirty sounds perfect,
Of course I can handle a band saw, I took shop
in junior high, My parents accept me for who I am, so they
should be intrigued by my new friend with the pierced tongue.
Isn't this why we want to take risks, why we love art,
why we have one more drink, why we hate compromise,
why we want to stop apologizing –
to earn the freedom to live passionately,
to flirt with the option to ruin our own life?

The Song You Sang to Me

Say anything you must and sail on,
but please don't say "You're history."
I did not change the course of your life
in a single moment, make *Besame, Besame mucho*
pulse in your brain every time I appeared,
Como se fuera esta noce la ultima vez,
I did not illuminate for you the shady way
through the garden of forking paths,
I did not shape your future,
I was not ever your Spanish Armada,
Que tengo miedo perdite, perdite despues,
It wasn't as if you had lowered your flag,
and the bloodlines and waterways all became mine
and it wasn't as if, had our lips never touched,
Quiero tenerte muy cerca, mirarme en tus ojos,
the Brit king and queen would be dark-eyed
and olive-skinned, and the pubs
from Inverness down to Dover
and over to Killarney would resound
with *Arriba, Abajo, Al Centro, Adentro!*
It wasn't as if we came together
when men shielded their hearts with armor,
when Goodbye! meant God be with you
and protect you as I would if I could,
Piensa que tal vez mañana
Yo ya estare muy lejos, muy lejos de ti.
It isn't as if the song you heard
was the song you sang to me.

Treason

That prominent scholar and beautiful man
I saw only in your photo of him.
I shared a joy with him and that is you.
He did not know what I knew.
I grew to value whatever gifts I drew
in the lottery of intimacies,
knowing that a view of me
in a stranger's eyes without my shirt,
flexing and full of triumph,
in every ironic context
of age and death and treason,
would be the price for playing the game
and loving it beyond reason.

The Object of the Crime

In 1911, Vincenzo Peruggia stole the Mona Lisa.

What kind of lover are you?
To me, you look like a little field mouse
I can hardly see in the shade of a great olive tree.
A cloud would have to cover the whole sky to dim
my memory of Vincenzo, who was better than good,
who was so ardent an amateur that he was professional.

He wore the artist smock that was the uniform
of Louvre guards. He fooled them all
because he really was an artist.
I smile inside when I think of what he did for me.
No visa granted him safe passage crossing any border.

He walked, bees swarmed, flowers bloomed,
the Alps diminished underneath his steady tread,
the Matterhorn was backdrop, glacial lakes, rivers,
the forests of pines, and finally the wheat fields.
I lay in a trunk, I will confide to you,
for a couple of years and napped
while my consort went mad with his secret passion,
until he could no longer hide
the jewel of his obsession,
and only then was I recognized for what I am.

And then La Giaconda toured Italia like a rite of spring,
her regal journey of Il Patria, destined then
to be enshrined forever, ruling crowds who wait on line
to see her through the highest quality, most translucent lens.
Some who see me say I look a little smug,
like someone who has been flattered,
like someone fertile, someone who might be pregnant,
in any case, someone satisfied with her importance.
These people are envious and they should be.

I like to think of his interview in jail,
his prize returned to its foreign home,
his sense of wounded righteousness,
waiting for the perfect question
to which he could respond "poetic license."

I am the object,
you voyeur en passant,
you collector of lessons from artifacts,
you self-conscious seeker of the timeless,
of The Crime of the Century.

Amuse me with a story, *per favore*,
of the law that you would break for love.

The Blindness of Trees

Maybe asteroids crash into Earth from intolerable loneliness.
- Kenneth Rosen, CavanKerry Blog; April 17, 2013

At first, I am too full of sadness
for the blindness of trees to respond.
The thousand green fingers waving
aimlessly in the wind, reaching up and out and
away from gravity's pull, oblivious to their own
endearing symmetry, anchored, bark-bound,
numbered in the forest like hairs of the head,
perch of a billion billing and bumbling birds,
rooted among the beautiful crawlers, the
wrigglers through ooze, and the segmented
ancient ones, all of whom have eyes of some
sort, however vestigial or still on the come,
despisers of fire, that elegant, seasonal
cleanser, beyond any scream painful,
muted and mooted and deaf as well,
mum to the owl's howl, cat's yowl,
barn fowl's gobble and cackle, but,
upon second thought, I find mercy
in blindness for trees, who feel asteroids
tragically dashing themselves on their
mineral kin as just another thud,
curious, absent the torture of love,
what the reason for anything is,
for the standing around, not unpleasantly
bound to a circling insouciant sun,
storing up pollen to fling in an ecstatic void.

To Diana

Into the horizon's slow wave the huge, red sun is sinking.
Soon the leaves are falling like a dark snow around us
and the wind lies along the beach pressing against a swollen tide.
We sit together high on the throne of an ancient feeling.
At the rim of our hearing, Leonidas' body falls at Thermopylae.
Archimedes opens his mouth to shout,
a breeze rustles the sails off Aulis, and always
the great barrier reef is breathing, building, wrestling with the sea.
A fire-fly in the distance, Krakatoa opens a red eye.
Over broken Sausalito the waters close easily.
Frozen among the ascending air bubbles
numberless as prayers or dreams,
San Francisco's blinded street lamps hang like pearls.
It is a very quiet moment.
All the silly kings who ever live
will mean to say what I will say to you.

The Fossil Record

Because of its accessibility and abundance of fossils, this rock section has been selected as the Global Boundary Stratotype Section and Point (GBSSP) representing the line between the Precambrian and the Cambrian period, 541.0 ± 1.0 million years ago.

-- loosely, from "Fortune Head," *Wikipedia*

Have you noticed in your travels, Kayla Jean,
(scholars, don't bother – it's a nom de poeme;
she loved her privacy and so did I)
have you noticed how the smooth promontories,
the upheaved, overgrown shoreline cliffs
and the inclines – so gradually sloped these days
they do not even slow your steps – are where the seismic,
volcanic and flood-torn events that have shaped
the history and meaning of life on earth lie quietly preserved?
When you were the temporary English department
secretary and I was a teaching fellow, young
and exemplary, we did a radical thing. We drove
ten miles to the next town for lunch. No one,
you said, had ever proposed driving so far for a little
different cuisine; for me, no one had so much stoked up
my glamour simply for coming from anywhere else.
You made my affordable auto a limousine and the moment
I have of you standing in dark blouse and white slacks,
posing purposefully, looking back
over your shoulder at camera man me
is undoubtedly the most erotic formation
in the Early Midwestern era of my geology.
The odds of your randomly reading this poem
are infinitesimal, like any particular earth tremor
prior to fact, like unlikely partners
meeting where roads cross. I am sure of it:
somewhere you are a grandmother,
having loved and been loved deeply.
I like to think we've done many things better
because of that cowgirl summer you rode on my back
as I breast-stroked the sunlit pool's full measure.
It was right for you to sleep with your boyfriend
before you shared a night with me. Who and how
you were we both knew and accepted, even
as we were incandescent, almost consumed
within each other's arms, flesh to flesh
and lava flowing through.

Washing Dishes

What could be more banal
than the drive to the metro
to pick up your mate?
The nominal reward, unless
it's really cold or raining hard,
is the kind of kiss you get
for undertaking minor inconveniences.
My father made that daily drive for years.
Working the night shift,
he got up in the early afternoon
so all the repetitious household chores
were done when he would meet her.
For him, in Brooklyn, it was an act
of embarrassment and contrition
because my mother had to work,
even though she really wanted to,
and even though it was a longer walk
than she could manage at day's end.

Today, in Takoma Park, it is sunny
and cool, the October leaves still green
as days shorten and the summer
leans indifferently towards fall.
Your call interrupts my writing.
You would just as soon stroll home,
but I can be there in eight minutes
and I will. I have my reasons.
I wonder what the life is of this poem.
Trains and calls will change,
and work, and attitudes,
and maybe even seasons.
What an apron string is immortality.
I always will remember how my father
gave to love a definition, washing dishes
carefully as choosing words,
and waiting for the phone to ring.

Nazar

> To welcome your return,
> in which I express my gratitude, to the Nth degree,
> for your neato (viz.) gift of *The New Shorter Oxford English Dictionary*

Upon your kiss, I slip indeed my natterjack identity.
I don a cappa magna sewn of nebrises and nutria, step softly
to your bath and place the nuphar carefully afloat, then
set the celadon dish of nard upon a stool within your reach.
Around the moist room, I arrange the num-nums
and, specifically, the Natal plums for nuncheon.
I can see, can taste, the water beading on your supine nuque.

I contemplate your nascence, like to think it could have been
prognosticated from my need for you as certainly
as nebulium from those nagging anomalous lines
in the spectra of nebulae, notwithstanding
that clump of ning-nongs and numps
among scions of science who thought they could triumph
denying transitions in N and O ions. A nunky at a nundine
would put nuppence on a scale for their wares.
It seems very sad to me that a life can come and go nugaciously,
no notion of noshi nor nostos to keep nominalism
from pounding one's head as a nebelwerfer would.
Minus you, I would be nescient of neroli,
nuddling along, worse – a nug, nullibiety.

I will linger longingly on the numerous nummies
nutant from my lips along the fragrant flesh
of your intremities, because, to whatever nerite
or nerkish existence I afterwards return,
I could always lie in my living room, couchant upon
a sloped stack of numnahs like some nunatak,
and nuncupate to myself, to eternity,
but really to you, the Nusselt number
of you know what and you know where.

End of Day Poem

wash the dishes whose no longer edible jewelry dries as I lie here
turn over drape my lazy arm along my most beloved sleeper
ring up my newest illicit lover to talk in the depth of this night
touch myself and imagine my very inventive mate and complicit lover
pleasuring each other primarily as a gift to me of course
okay I already did that anyway let's just get on thank you
yes children created multi-tasking in my generation
but my job is showing that neither their clever achievement
and especially not the sad ransom paid for it
are digital that is the last aside let's just get on thank you
open the novel whose author is speaker at Advocacy Day next week
start the search update that tedious abstract my resume
enter the online insomniac chat room of souls drifting jellyfish
dictate the letters to lost loves I still care for
pick out the suit shirt tie shoes for tomorrow
email my senator please stop this counterproductive war now
listen I learned from young lovers in bed all night long
that the birds will start singing in darkness to bring on the dawn
and the dawn is that ritual kiss on each eyelid
the death of whatever a moment ago was most dear
then the curtain's up sweet stuff let's just get on thank you
I make you one promise to never forget all the other things
you could be doing my precious the insight of charity
writing the check you could think of a cure
you could see in your mind how the garden would look
if you planted the irises not in a row
if I ever for even a moment thought this here and now
in the mirror of your face and mine were not fertile
immersion reflection recombinant god I sincerely
do not know what I would do write me your poem
this tragic and merry-go-round world is yours to make holy
bless you for letting me be who I am
the birds my love are singing all the other deeds
we might have done are gone let's get on now thank you

End of Day Poem II

At the end of this day
I am only writing this poem
because I wouldn't want to have written
only one end of day poem
as if the end of each and every day were not
its own and particular creation
with its singular memorable colors and shape
and textures that look like one texture
as time shimmies its little undulation
into distance. I wouldn't want
to have gone back to sleep
when I got this idea
and to have awakened without it
any more than I might not have asked
you back to my place
at the end of that day long ago
It was not anyone or anyplace
It was so particular with its bottle
of wine from Thrifty's
Has there ever been more of a red
in a glass at the end of a day
It was that day and this day
not a day or any day.
This poem is just to say
you are in my life
that primary color like which there is
even though in and around
such a rainbow of ribbons
is bending to haul in and fling out the light
no other
as this day is ending and that night surrounds.

Ivy

If your love should ever leave, my heart would stall,
would flutter like a bird's wings below the eave,
no word I could utter would suffice for solace
and all that sings in poetry would be muted
like ivy suddenly uprooted, frozen to a wall.

Your Love Poem

To love me now, you would have to want to kiss
my favorite orifices, really kiss,
meaning not in reminiscence. I will return to this.
The sight of my now thinning hair as wild as it is
in morning after all the tossings of our night
would have to seem to you endearing
and when I interrupt and say, "Repeat that, please,"
you would have to feel that anything
was worthwhile saying over just for me.
You would have to want to be the one
who lifts the toilet top to see what bent
or broke from so much flushing;
you would have to want your hand
to hold my stomach when I throw up;
after the operation,
you would have to want to put your lips
on the warm bruises and your tongue on the stitches
both to see how they feel in your own mouth
and to soothe what is possible to soothe;
you would have to love my every scar
and cut and abrasion and the lump
from bumping the chair; you would have
to want to touch every part of my body
just to make connection with your own,
smooth or hairy you would have to want
to make it yours, and every blemish and
every discoloration and every aberration
from normality would have to remind you
how much you like to think
that only you could love these,
and you would even have to know
that that idea was fiction,
others could and had,
and when you read of love so great that age
cannot wither nor custom stale her infinite
variety and how sorrows of the changing face
are loved, and the love of bare, ruined choirs

where late the sweet birds sang,
you would have to think of me;
you would have to know in your bones
no laceration, no amputation,
no crash or fall, no rheumy eye, no hobbled gait
of mine or yours would mar the body of our love,
or dim your wish to serve me when I need you most.
Most difficult of all, you would have to love me
always in the moment; notwithstanding all we shared
of pleasure and of strife that's seeped into our blood,
you know I'd be insulted to be loved in memory.
To love me now,
you would have to love me as I love you.

Acknowledgments

With thanks to my family and friends for their caring natures, humor and encouragement.

"To Diana" has appeared previously in *Beloit Poetry Review*
"Bluets" has appeared previously in *The Midwest Quarterly.*

C&R PRESS CHAPBOOKS

C&R Press hosts two chapbook selection periods from June to September and November to March coupled with a reading in New York City each year. The Winter Soup Bowl and Summer Tide Pool Chapbook Series are open to new and established writers in poetry, fiction, essay and other creative writing.

2016 SUMMER TIDE POOL SELECTIONS

Cuntstruck
by Kate Northrop

Relief Map
by Erin M. Bertram

Love Undefined
by Jonathan Katz

2016 Winter Soup Bowl

Notes from the Negro Side of the Moon
by Earl Braggs

A Hunger Called Music: A Verse History in Black Music
by Meredith Nnoka

OTHER C&R PRESS TITLES

FICTION

Ivy vs. Dogg
by Brian Leung

A History of the Cat In Nine Chapters or Less
by Anis Shivani

While You Were Gone
by Sybil Baker

Spectrum
by Martin Ott

That Man in Our Lives
by Xu Xi

SHORT FICTION

Meditations on the Mother Tongue
by An Tran

The Protester Has Been Released
by Janet Sarbanes

ESSAY AND CREATIVE NONFICTION

Immigration Essays
by Sybil Baker

Je suis l'autre: Essays and Interrogations
by Kristina Marie Darling

Death of Art
by Chris Campanioni

POETRY

Negro Side of the Moon
by Early Braggs

Holdfast
by Christian Anton Gerard

Ex Domestica
by E.G. Cunningham

Collected Lies and Love Poems
by John Reed

Imagine Not Drowning
by Kelli Allen

Les Fauves
by Barbara Crooker

Tall as You are Tall Between Them
by Annie Christain

The Couple Who Fell to Earth
by Michelle Bitting

CHAPBOOKS

Cuntstruck by Kate Northrop
Relief Map by Erin Bertram
A Hunger Called Music: A Verse History in Black Music
by Meredith Nnoka

CPSIA information can be obtained
at www.ICGtesting.com
Printed in the USA
BVHW031542191220
594987BV00008B/14

9 781936 196562